Tips for the
READING
TEAM
Strategies
for Tutors

BARBARA J. WALKER
Oklahoma State University
Stillwater, Oklahoma, USA

LESLEY MANDEL MORROW
Rutgers, The State University of New Jersey
New Brunswick, New Jersey, USA

Editors

INTERNATIONAL READING ASSOCIATION
800 Barksdale Road, PO Box 8139
Newark, Delaware 19714-8139, USA
www.reading.org

The International Reading Association attempts, through its publications, to provide a forum for a wide spectrum of opinions on reading. This policy permits divergent viewpoints without implying the endorsement of the Association.

Director of Publications Joan M. Irwin
Assistant Director of Publications Jeanette K. Moss
Editor-in-Chief, Books Christian A. Kempers
Senior Editor Matthew W. Baker
Assistant Editor Janet S. Parrack
Assistant Editor Mara P. Gorman
Publications Coordinator Beth Doughty
Association Editor David K. Roberts
Production Department Manager Iona Sauscermen
Art Director Boni Nash
Electronic Publishing Supervisor Wendy A. Mazur
Electronic Publishing Specialist Anette Schütz-Ruff
Electronic Publishing Specialist Cheryl J. Strum
Electronic Publishing Assistant Peggy Mason

Project Editor Mara P. Gorman

Library of Congress Cataloging in Publication Data
Walker, Barbara J., 1946–
   Tips for the Reading Team: Strategies for Tutors/Barbara J. Walker, Lesley Mandel Morrow.
      p.   cm.
   Includes bibliographical references (p.   ).
   1. Reading (Elementary).   2. Tutors and tutoring.   I. Morrow, Lesley Mandel.   II. Title.
LB1573.W312   1998   98-42337
372.4--dc21
ISBN 0-87207-190-1 (pbk.)
Second printing, August 2001

Contents

Introduction / 1

SECTION I

Motivating Readers / 7

SECTION II

Storybook Reading / 16

SECTION III

Reading Together and Rereading / 28

SECTION IV

Figuring Out Words / 38

SECTION V

Supporting Understanding / 53

SECTION VI

Frameworks for Tutoring Young
Children to Read / 76

Conclusion / 85

The Reading Teacher Article
Reference List / 88

Introduction

IN RESPONSE TO the America Reads Challenge, and the increasing emphasis on using volunteer tutors to help all children learn to read, we have created a series of publications to help tutors understand and mentor young children. Volunteer tutors can provide the personal support that will keep students engaged in literacy tasks, but they need to work as part of a collaborative team. To be effective, tutors need to have some training and work alongside reading specialists and classroom teachers. We propose the volunteer tutors use a tutoring program like the one found in our first publication on this topic *The Reading Team: A Handbook for Volunteer Tutors K–3*.

This book was developed to complement *The Reading Team* by providing instructional tips for teachers and tutors who are collaboratively developing volunteer tutoring programs for struggling readers in the early grades. This compilation of research-based teaching procedures taken from articles in the International Reading Association journal *The Reading Teacher* is designed for use by both the reading specialist or supervisor who is working with volunteer tutors and the tutors themselves.

A thorough description of the tutoring session is included in *The Reading Team*, but we will outline it here as well:

- This program includes a time for reading old favorites that are easy books, stories, or poems that children know well.

- After beginning with old favorites, the tutor and child together read a book that will provide some challenge. This may be a predictable book or a classroom text that the student's teacher has given the tutor. We suggest that the tutor read to the child or that they read together and discuss the book thoroughly, and that the tutor offers support and guidance when necessary. At this time, the focus will be on understanding the reading selection.

- We also suggest that the tutor and child write together, exchanging ideas on paper.

- Each session can contain a time to read for enjoyment during which both the tutor and the child choose books to read for their own individual purposes.

- The tutor and child also choose an interesting word, place it on a chart, and discuss aspects of the word such as the meaning, the letters, and the word pattern.

- Finally, the tutor and the child discuss the success of the session and write down what they did on a chart.

To make the tips in this book easy to apply to the tutoring session described in *The Reading Team*, we have created a
symbol illustrating where each strategy fits in the session:

Read Old Favorites

Read Together

Write Together

Read for Enjoyment

Talk About Words

Summarize Success

You will find these symbols in the margins of this book to indicate where a tip may best be used. Thus volunteer tutors can use this book as a quick reference guide to get ideas for their tutoring sessions. Keep in mind, however, that some of these suggestions also apply to the entire session. We suggest that new tutors read through the entire book to get some general ideas they can use.

Reading specialists, tutor trainers, and classroom teachers who are working closely with tutors can help tutors identify specific techniques they can use to adapt the tutoring procedures to the specific needs of their students. Teachers, in particular, understand the specific needs of children in their classrooms and can suggest alternative procedures to tutors. Tutors who are working alone can use the symbols and introductory information to help them decide if the tip would promote greater reading engagement.

When we finished *The Reading Team* and decided to write a guidebook for tutors that included specific activities, we decided that *The Reading Teacher* provided a wonderful source of easily adapted teaching procedures. We ourselves often have relied on articles from *The Reading Teacher* to augment our own teaching. To write the book, we gathered articles from 1985 to 1997. Although many of the articles deal with classroom instruction, we have adapted specific articles for use in a tutoring situation. Many classroom teaching procedures are just as appropriate for tutoring sessions involving readers who are at risk.

This book is divided into six sections. Section I presents general principles that develop motivation for learning. These principles will help tutors develop a positive relationship with the children they mentor and will enable tutors to help children learn to like reading. Section II contains various procedures for reading storybooks with young children. It describes ways tutors can embellish the "Read Together" aspect of the tutoring session described in *The Reading Team*. In Section III, several methods of promoting reading fluency are presented including reading together and rereading. Section IV describes procedures to help young children think about and figure out difficult words using multiple strategies, thus increasing children's ability to decode words when reading. Section V presents methods of supporting understanding, such as extending background knowledge and using self-questioning. Section VI describes other tutoring programs. Many of the frameworks of these programs are similar to those described in *The Reading Team* but each provides new procedures and principles to enhance the tutoring session.

It is our hope that this book will add abundant techniques to your growing tutoring repertoire.

Motivating Readers

Key Factors in Reading Motivation
from "Creating Classroom Cultures That Foster Reading Motivation" by Linda B. Gambrell

Classroom Interactions That Motivate
from "What Students Say About Motivating Experiences in a Whole Language Classroom" by Penny Oldfather

Reading for Meaning
from "Building Communities of Readers and Writers" by Trevor Cairney and Susan Langbien

Open-Ended Reading Activities
from "How Literacy Tasks Influence Children's Motivation for Literacy" by Julianne Turner and Scott Paris

Engaging Children With Print
from "Making Difficult Books Accessible and Easy Books Acceptable" by Linda Fielding and Cathy M. Roller

Key Factors in Reading Motivation

RELUCTANT READERS OFTEN need encouragement from both teachers and tutors to engage their interest in reading. In her September 1996 article entitled, "Creating Classroom Cultures That Foster Reading Motivation," Linda B. Gambrell discusses six factors that are related to increased motivation to read. Tutors can consider these factors when creating lesson plans and planning their tutoring environment. Understanding the importance of modeling, access to books, student choice, and tutor-student interaction is a first step toward tutoring success.

Strategies

➤ Tutors are an explicit reading model. The adult who values reading and shares his or her love of reading with children will motivate children to read. These individuals often talk about what they are reading and use their current reading as a way to demonstrate reading strategies.

➤ Tutors can create a book-rich environment. Increasing the number of books available for children to read increases the quality of reading experiences which in turn increases motivation.

➤ Tutors can create opportunities for choice. Books that children find most interesting to read are those they have selected for their own reasons and purposes.

➤ Tutors provide children opportunities to interact socially with others. Children often comment that they chose a book and found it interesting because their tutor told them about it. Sharing books with friends and tutors is an important factor in developing motivated readers.

➤ Tutors can provide children with opportunities to become familiar with many books. Children are curious about and more motivated to read books that are familiar.

➤ Tutors can provide appropriate reading-related incentives. Rewards that are related strongly to reading and reading behavior, especially books, but also bookmarks and praise, can be effective in increasing motivation.

Classroom Interactions That Motivate

ANOTHER ARTICLE THAT addresses factors in motivating children to read is titled, "What Students Say About Motivating Experiences in a Whole Language Classroom" from May 1993. In it, Penny Oldfather suggests key characteristics of interactions that contributed to increasing motivation in a classroom setting. Students said they liked reading and writing when their voices were honored, when they made choices about what and how to learn, and when they became personally invested in their literacy. Tutors can use these skills to get to know the children with whom they work and to learn more about the children's reading habits.

Strategies

Four aspects were critical to the children in this study.

➤ Tutors can encourage self-expression as they invite perspectives and honor individual opinions. Ask students questions about their reading and listen carefully to their answers.

➤ Tutors can focus on children's personal understanding. Children learn to share their growing understandings about the topics they are studying.

➤ Tutors can allow children many choices within the well-established structures and requirements of the tutoring session, including reading picture books, newspapers, poetry, and their own writing.

➤ A responsive tutor is a key to motivation. Responsive tutors listen and respond to children, openly share feelings, and are enthusiastic about learning. They also share power, responsibility, and enthusiasm with their tutees.

Reading for Meaning

ONE OF THE responsibilities of a tutor is to help children see reading as a meaningful activity that is an important part of everyday life. In their April 1989 article, "Building Communities of Readers and Writers," Trevor Cairney and Susan Langbien suggest that although reading and writing are natural extensions of young children's lives, in school children often learn that reading is a teacher-centered, textbook-dominated activity. To motivate children, reading and writing need to be purposeful activities. Tutors can help provide students with reading activities and opportunities for discussion that illustrate the relevance of reading.

Strategies

1. Reading and writing are cultural activities and are extensions of people's day-to-day cultural lives.

- Each day tutors can discuss what they have read, such as newspapers, phone books, letters, or bills, and discuss what they have written, such as checks, friends' phone numbers, or messages to friends.
- Tutors and teachers need to ask themselves: "How significant is literacy within the life of my classroom?" and "How important is literacy within the lives of the children I teach?"

2. The following guidelines for reading with children will help them understand the importance of reading as a daily activity:

- Make sure the book is not too hard, but just right.
- Don't interrupt students; let them read to the end of the sentence.
- Give students plenty of time to self-correct a word.

- Prompt students to understand what they are reading rather than focusing on letters or words.
- Make sure they read, read, read.

3. Social interaction directly influences the meaning we make as we read and write. For example, if reading is done simply to fill out a workbook page, then children read with different purposes than if they discuss the story with a group of peers or

their tutor. Tutors can provide children with a new reason to read by encouraging them to discuss their everyday reading.

4. When reading with children, tutors can elaborate topics introduced by a child or they can ask children to clarify what they said. These social processes motivate children to read.

Open-Ended Reading Activities

IN THEIR MAY 1995 article "How Literacy Tasks Influence Children's Motivation for Literacy," Julianne Turner and Scott Paris suggest that open-ended literacy tasks motivate students to read because they provide appropriate challenges and opportunities to collaborate with others. Open-ended activities are those that allow student choice, do not have right or wrong answers, and give students the chance to solve problems.

Strategies

The following aspects of open-ended activities are recommended for use by tutors:

➤ Provide choice during literacy instruction by making sure you have a number of books with you or have access to the school classroom or library. Children can choose books for oral reading activities and sustained silent reading.

➤ Create moderately challenging tasks that will lead to positive feelings because students make new discoveries. One example of a challenging task that all students can accomplish successfully is the text scramble. Take text from stories or poems your tutee has read and with which you know he or she is familiar. Separate the sentences into individual words and allow the student to reconstruct each sentence in a meaningful way.

➤ Open tasks require students to think strategically and to monitor their learning. These tasks do not have one right way of doing things. For example, have students paste strips of text from a favorite story in sequence and then illustrate the accompanying text.

➤ Opportunities to learn from and with others is extremely motivating. Comments and ideas can pique students' curiosity and spark further interest. Examples of appropriate comments include prompts (Does this have an *s* in it?), coaching (Does this make sense? I think you need to go back), and asking the student for help (Do you know how to spell *listen?*).

➤ Open literacy tasks support children to make sense of their learning. When reading activities focus on making sense of the text, children are motivated because they are solving interesting problems. These challenges result in personal growth.

Engaging Children With Print

TUTORS OFTEN WORK with at-risk readers who have little familiarity with books. This lack of familiarity means that it is often difficult to get these children excited about reading. In their May 1992 article, "Making Difficult Books Accessible and Easy Books Acceptable" Linda Fielding and Cathy M. Roller discuss ways to engage at-risk readers with print. During free-choice reading, at-risk children often do not read because they do not know how to find a book that they can read, there is no book available that they can read, or they do not want to read the easy books they are able to read. This article suggests ways both to help these children with challenging books and increase their interest in easier books.

Strategies

Making Difficult Books Accessible

Children need to read interesting books appropriate to conceptual development but they often choose to read books that are too difficult. This choice is a sign of motivation to read but can lead to frustration. Tutors can help make difficult books accessible in the following ways:

- *Allow independent reading time.* Children can have positive interactions around difficult books if they are allowed to explore them at their own pace. Sometimes they can find interesting information in these books.

- *Read to children.* Less-able readers need to hear the language and vocabulary of more difficult books. Reading to these students allows them access to the more complex ideas and language in these books.

- *Reread.* When children read a passage repeatedly, the reread passage not only becomes easier, but children are able to read new passages at about the same difficulty level.

- *Precede difficult books with easier books.* Reading an easier book about the same topic shows children what they already know and gives them a chance to encounter technical words about the topic in a familiar context.

Making Easy Books Acceptable

Children often refuse to read easy books and hold deep prejudices against them. They want to keep up with other students at their level and they find easy books uninteresting.

- *Model use and enjoyment of easy books.* Tutors can demonstrate to children that they read easy books in their own adult lives. Most of the pleasure reading adults do is easy.

- *Alter purposes for easy reading.* Having children prepare to read the easy book to a younger child in a local day-care center or a younger brother or sister makes easy books acceptable.

- *Tape books.* Having children make a tape for another child encourages students to choose easy books so they can sound good on the tape.

- *Challenge preconceptions about easy books.* Picture books appeal to children and adults of all ages. They can easily be part of the literary selections in tutoring sessions. Book-sharing sessions can illustrate the complexity of the themes of easy picture books.

- *Broaden the concept of acceptable reading.* Use many genres that are short yet interesting. The same predictable, repetitive features can be found in poems, songs, raps, cheers, and in children's own writing.

- *Make nonfiction available.* Much about science and history can be learned from easy-to-read children's books that have diagrams to illustrate more complex ideas.

Storybook Reading

Reading With Children
from "Interactive Experiences With Storybook Reading" by Dorothy S. Strickland and Lesley Mandel Morrow

Reading Aloud to Encourage Involvement
from "Engaging With Reading Through Interactive Read-Alouds" by Shelby J. Barrentine

Read-Aloud Strategies for Children Who Have English as a Second Language
from "Story Reading With Limited English Speaking Children in the Regular Classroom" by Ruth A. Hough, Joanne R. Nurss, and D. Scott Enright

Strategies for Interactive Storybook Reading
from "Interactive Storybook Reading for At-Risk Learners" by Jannell P. Klesius and Priscilla L. Griffith

Involving Children With Print
from "Sharing Big Books" by Dorothy S. Strickland and Lesley Mandel Morrow

Reading With Children

MANY CHILDREN WHO need tutoring have had little experience with storybook reading. They may not have been read to very often. In their January 1989 article, "Interactive Experiences With Storybook Reading," Dorothy S. Strickland and Lesley Mandel Morrow suggest that reading to children increases their interest in books and in learning to read. Children who have been read to associate reading with pleasure and imitate those who read to them. Tutors can use a few simple strategies to help them prepare for reading to their students. The authors present an outline for storybook reading that actively encourages listener participation.

Strategies

Prepare Questions for Discussion

Before you read a story, look at the book with the child, explaining what you are going to do: "Today I am going to read a story called *The Little Red Hen*. Let's look at the pictures to see if you can tell what it's going to be about." Turn the pages of the book, allowing the child to explore it and ask questions before you read. Ask the child to think about the story using specific questions and statements such as, "As I read, decide if the little red hen is doing the right thing."

Read the Story

1. Rehearse ahead of time.

2. Show illustrations as you read.

3. Pause at natural breaks for the child's reactions, comments, or questions.

4. Ask questions and model responses, keeping in mind your immediate objective, which is to help the child understand the meaning of the story. You can do this by asking questions such as "Can you remember what help the little red hen has had so far? How have the other animals acted about giving help?" If the child does not respond, change the questions to statements: "These animals aren't very helpful to the little red hen. Each time she asks for help the animals all answer 'Not I.'"

5. Ask the child to predict what will happen next and reinforce her responses.

Discuss After Reading

Guide the discussion with leading questions such as "Do you think the little red hen did the right thing? What would you have done? What did you learn?"

Extend Your Interactive Reading

- Have the child chant repetitive phrases from the story along with you.
- Pause before predictable phrases, letting the child fill them in.
- Have the child retell the story.
- Use feltboards with story characters to model retelling the story, then let the child retell the story.

You can encourage the child's retelling by using prompts: In the beginning... or Who were the characters?

Reading Aloud to Encourage Involvement

READING ALOUD TO children may seem like a passive activity for them, and many tutors may be concerned that this time is not productive. However, in many classrooms, the purpose of reading aloud has shifted from simply being viewed as "down time" to include more instructional purposes. Teachers read aloud to convey information, to teach literature-based math lessons, and to demonstrate reading processes. Tutors also can use reading aloud to engage their students and to get them actively thinking and learning. Dissatisfied with straight-through storybook reading, Shelby J. Barrentine suggests ways to help increase student involvement during read-alouds in the September 1996 article, "Engaging With Reading Through Interactive Read-Alouds."

Strategies

To use interactive read-alouds, consider the following general strategies:

➤ Begin by reviewing the illustrations and inviting predictions. Ask the child to justify her predictions: "What

makes you think this story takes place in the country? Why do you think the mother and daughter will make a pie?"

➤ As you read, invite brief interactions about what is happening in the story as well as what characters might be feeling.

➤ During the reading of the story, temper lengthy interactions and save them for a postreading discussion. However, allow the child to discuss connections between her own life and the story.

➤ As you read, demonstrate and support conversations about story structure and reading strategies. For example, ask the child to compare the actions of the different characters to encourage her to see similarities and differences.

The following suggestions are helpful when planning an interactive read-aloud:

➤ Select high-interest picture books with rich language, absorbing plots, and lively characters. Before reading aloud, read the book several times to yourself.

➤ Identify appropriate places to ask your student "What do you think will happen?" These include critical points in the story, where a problem or conflict arises for the characters.

➤ Anticipate where you may need to build the child's background knowledge. Does the story contain references or words that will be unfamiliar to your student? Be prepared to address this information and decide in advance where in the text you will do so.

➤ Think through how you will phrase your questions and anticipate responses.

➤ After you have planned the read-aloud event, be prepared to relinquish your plans. Be responsive to the child and tailor your responses to his or her statements.

➤ After reading, devise opportunities for the child to explore stories in personal and exciting ways. Ask the student to share related stories from her own experience, draw a picture in response to the story, or act out a scene from the story.

Read-Aloud Strategies for Children Who Have English as a Second Language

SOME TUTORS WILL work with students for whom English is not a native language. Although many strategies for helping these students are the same as those listed in the other excerpts in this book, the February 1986 article, "Story Reading With Limited English Speaking Children in the Regular Classroom" by Ruth A. Hough, Joanne R. Nurss, and D. Scott Enright suggests common-sense procedures for reading stories to young English as a Second Language (ESL) children. The authors stress that story reading is pleasurable and helps low-experience students hear book language. These interactions help children develop English vocabulary, oral fluency, a sense of story, and concepts about print.

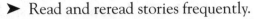

Effective Story Reading

➤ Read and reread stories frequently.

➤ Use verbal cueing strategies while reading: pause to indicate a change in events, exaggerate intonation to emphasize key words or concepts, change pitch and volume to indicate voices of different characters, and change volume to indicate a change in scene or character's mood.

➤ Use nonverbal cueing strategies: point to illustrations or parts of illustrations, use facial expressions to indicate characters or a change in a character's mood, and use gestures to accompany key actions or events in the story.

➤ Involve your student in the story by asking appropriate questions such as "Who is this?" or "What are they doing?"

➤ Select predictable books (ones that have a pattern, refrain, or predictable sequence). Encourage the child to repeat the refrain, to complete the sentence pattern once she knows it, and to predict new characters using illustrations.

➤ Select well-illustrated books because they provide an additional way to figure out words.

➤ Throughout the story, ask thought-provoking questions: "What just occurred? What might come next? Why do you think x will happen next? Can you project yourself into the story? How would you feel?"

Strategies for Interactive Storybook Reading

STUDIES HAVE SHOWN that children whose parents read to them at home acquire school literacy at an earlier age. Tutors can imitate the close interactions provided by at-home reading. In their April 1996 article, "Interactive Storybook Reading for At-Risk Learners," Jannell P. Klesius and Priscilla L. Griffith describe an approach to reading that parallels at-home experience. This flexible routine has an informal, conversational approach to talking about stories. Tutors participate in discussions by predicting what will happen next and sharing related personal experiences. The authors suggest a number of strategies.

Strategies

Questioning

➤ Ask open-ended questions that help children take an active role, such as "Why do you think the title might be?"

➤ Questions can engage the child: "Lesley, what do you see in the picture?"

➤ Prediction questions, for example "What will happen next?" help model how a reader uses information from past experiences. The student will see how her knowledge about details in pictures helps her predict what will happen next.

Scaffolding

Scaffolding is a term used in literacy instruction that means the gradual withdrawal of adult (for example, teacher or tutor) support using modeling, questioning, and feedback (see page 56 in Section V for a further discussion of scaffolding). To scaffold a child's learning is to encourage her to reach her own conclusions. In the case of reading aloud, allowing children to discuss the story helps them expand their ideas.

➤ Tutors can give explanations to clarify or share personal experiences.

➤ Tutors also can point out details in the illustrations that increase enjoyment and provide clues to understanding.

➤ When children offer responses, the tutors also can offer responses.

Ambiance

Praise establishes warmth. A tutor can encourage the child to sit close to him or her. This closeness allows the child to point out items in the pictures and discuss them.

Children's Talk

As children listen to the tutor reread familiar books, their discussion increases. They also begin to use adult behaviors to elaborate story understanding, such as using an illustration to retell a part of the story. Tutors can model adult behaviors that include

- clarifying information;
- talking about story elements, such as characters;
- drawing attention to illustrations;
- extending the child's responses;

- extending the child's vocabulary knowledge;
- praise;
- pointing out text features; and
- scaffolding strategies, such as using illustrations to figure out a word.

Involving Children With Print

ONE OF THE tools that classroom teachers use with their students is the Big Book. Big Books are enlarged versions of beginning reading books. Tutors can ask their tutee's teacher or school librarian to loan them Big Books for use during tutoring sessions. These books are useful because the type is very large and they usually are illustrated. In their January 1990 article entitled "Sharing Big Books," Dorothy S. Strickland and Lesley Mandel Morrow describe how using Big Books (or books with predictable language) is one of the most effective ways to get young children involved with print. They delineate key features of this approach and recommend instructional strategies.

Strategies

➤ Predictable language patterns are a key feature of Big Books. The predictability of the language makes it easy for young children to remember the words.

➤ Repeated readings make Big Books a rich resource for language activities. With each reading the child becomes more fluent and extends his or her understanding.

➤ After the first or second reading, track the print with your hand. This helps the child get a sense of the directionality of written language and the match of speech to print.

➤ Occasionally use the first reading as a demonstration of how readers think. Use statements, such as:

> I bet this story is about....
> I wonder what will happen next.
> I'm a little confused by....
> I'll keep reading to find out more.
> I would really feel...if I were....
> This reminds me of....
> Now I understand why....

➤ Involve your student in predicting words and phrases by pausing as you read aloud to let her fill in the anticipated language.

➤ After several readings of the text, you can focus the child's attention on features in the text, such as repeated words, initial letters of words, or punctuation marks. This helps her to learn to talk about reading and writing.

➤ Enlarged text helps young children understand and experience what it means to be a reader. You can send smaller versions of Big Books home for your student to read with her parents.

➤ You can write your own book with your student. Ideas for books include alphabet and number books; category books (for example, round things, red things, or soft things);

and informational books based on themes such as dinosaurs, spiders, or zoo animals.

➤ You also can write a book following the pattern of a predictable text. For example, you might use *The Three Little Pigs* to make a story titled *The Three Little Goats*.

Reading Together and Rereading

Reading to Become Fluent
from "Fluency for Everyone: Incorporating Fluency Instruction in the Classroom" by Timothy V. Rasinski

Rereading: Reading Books Again
from "Repeated Reading: Research Into Practice" by Sarah L. Dowhower

Paired Reading
from "Peer Tutoring and Paired Reading: Combining Two Powerful Techniques" by Keith Topping

Poetry and Paired Reading
from "Shared Poetry: A Whole Language Experience Adapted for Remedial Readers" by LaDonna K. Wicklund

Choral Reading
from "Using Choral Reading to Promote Language Learning for ESL Students" by Joyce K. McCauley and Daniel S. McCauley

Reading to Become Fluent

ONE OF THE goals of tutoring students who are struggling to learn to read is to help them read more fluently. Fluent reading is characterized by reading meaningful phrases smoothly and easily with expression. Tutors can use familiar texts and modeling to promote fluent reading. In his May 1989 article, "Fluency For Everyone: Incorporating Fluency Instruction in the Classroom," Timothy V. Rasinski outlines a number of methods that have been used effectively to promote fluent reading. Tutors can use these methods in isolation or in combination.

Strategies

➤ Fluency is promoted when children read text that they find relatively easy. Tutors need to have plenty of easy reading material available during their tutoring sessions. They can ask their student's teacher or librarian for help in finding this material. Tutors also need to allow their student time to read independently during each session.

➤ Tutors should not be afraid to have students read the same material repeatedly and often, especially if they like it. Repetition is essential to achieving fluency. Have your student reread books.

➤ Model what fluent reading sounds like. Children need frequent opportunities to see and hear fluent reading.

Read good literature aloud for the student so he or she hears fluent reading. Read together to model fluent reading.

➤ Talk directly about the aspects of fluency to improve this skill. Remind your student to listen to your expression and pauses as you read orally. Discuss these factors to heighten the student's sensitivity to what is means to be fluent.

➤ Give feedback to your student. Tell him how he is doing, praising any aspects of fluent reading that you hear.

➤ Support your student by having him listen to a fluently read passage at the same time he is reading it. Read slightly ahead of the child and then phase out, letting the child take the lead. Tape-recorded passages also support children's fluent reading. In this format, the child can work on fluency independently by listening and reading along with the tape several times.

➤ Fluency involves reading chunks or phrases of text. Remind your student that the text is written in meaningful phrases. Read passages in which the phrase boundaries are marked with a pencil slash. Occasionally read poems, famous speeches, or popular songs that have the phrases marked.

Rereading: Reading Books Again

To BECOME BETTER readers, children need to increase word recognition and comprehension. The more words children know, the easier it is for them to read, and the more they understand, the more they will enjoy reading. Tutors can use rereading of familiar passages to help children become better readers. In her March 1989 article "Repeated Reading: Research Into Practice," Sarah L. Dowhower reviews research showing that rereading passages improves reading and understanding. She suggests guidelines for practice that tutors can use in their sessions.

Strategies

Guidelines for Rereading

There are general procedural tips that tutors should keep in mind when using repeated readings.

1. Keep passages short (50–300 words). You can use passages from many different kinds of reading materials.

2. Keep the practice passages at the same level of difficulty until the child can read fluently. Your student's teacher can help you determine the difficulty level of the passages.

3. Don't be concerned with a high degree of shared words between the passages. Seeing words more than once will help your student learn them.

4. Use the read-along approach with the children who are reading word by word.

5. Students reach optimal fluency between three and five rereadings.

Supported Instruction in Rereading

1. Read the story to your student. Construct a story map and summary together. (A story map is a timeline showing the sequence of the story development. For further discussion of story maps see pages 57 to 66 in Section V.)

2. Next read together orally to develop oral reading fluency.

3. Finally, have your student practice a section of the text independently. When he or she reads it accurately with good expression, move on to the next story.

Additional Rereading Techniques

1. To use assisted procedures, provide a tape recorder, tape, and book. The child will keep a record of how many times he or she reads or listens to a book using a chart you design together.

2. To use unassisted procedures, provide a timing device, such as an hour glass or clock, and some books. The child can keep track of how fast he reads each time he practices a passage.

3. Once the child has become familiar with the book and feels he is ready, he reads the book to you or into a tape recorder.

4. If the child reads easily, he can receive a certificate you design, or a sticker.

5. The child chooses another book to start practicing.

Partner Reading

This strategy can be used by tutors who work with more than one student.

1. This is often called paired repeated reading. You can have students at the same reading level read as partners.

2. Each partner choose a 50-word passage and reads it silently.

3. One partner reads the passage aloud three times.

4. The students evaluate each other after each reading, talking about the improvement the student has made.

5. The children switch roles and repeat the sequence.

Paired Reading

READING TOGETHER INCREASES the amount of reading practice for young children, which in turn improves fluency. In his March 1989 article "Peer Tutoring and Paired Reading: Combining Two Powerful Techniques," Keith Topping discusses how the approaches mentioned in the title have been combined to produce reading gains for both the student being tutored and the tutor. The combination of peer tutoring and paired reading has more able readers reading alongside less able readers in classrooms. This strategy can be applied by adult tutors in tutoring sessions as well. Instead of working with a peer who is a more able reader, students work one on one with their adult tutor using the same techniques.

Strategies

1. Have the child choose books he wants to read.
2. Begin by reading together with the child
3. You and the child prearrange a nonverbal signal such as a nudge or a squeeze to indicate readiness to read alone. When the child feels able to read alone, he gives the signal.
4. When the child reads alone, support the reading by "phasing in" to read with the child, supplying a correct word when necessary.
5. Provide praise for fluent reading throughout the session.

Sessions should last at least 15 minutes and no longer than 30 minutes. You will need frequent access to the school library to select books. After the initial session have a feedback meeting with your student. Have him discuss, provide suggestions, and write comments about the experience. This will help you to know if you are providing adequate support to the student.

Poetry and Paired Reading

SELECTING APPROPRIATE READING material for their students is often a challenge for volunteer tutors. In the March 1989 article "Shared Poetry: A Whole Language Experience Adapted for Remedial Readers," LaDonna K. Wicklund suggests that poetry can be used to enhance word identification and fluency. Sharing poetry is highly motivating and offers struggling readers an opportunity to play and compose with language. By rereading poetry, children naturally learn the rhythmic sounds and rhyme of language. They also learn vocabulary in context. Wicklund suggests selecting poetry that is short and can be illustrated easily.

Strategies

1. Select a poem that is appropriate for the age, interests, and experience of the child. Good sources are Shel Silverstein's *Where the Sidewalk Ends* (1974) and Bill Martin's *Sounds of Language Readers* (1970).
2. Copy the poem on paper.

3. Read the poem aloud asking the child to listen for images in the poetry.

4. Discuss images with the child. You can ask questions such as "What did you see while I read this poem? What did you hear?"

5. Read the poem together while you point to individual words.

6. Read the poem several more times taking turns pointing to the individual words.

7. The child can illustrate a copy of the poem after you have read it or at home.

Extending the Lesson

Use the poem as a springboard for writing. Your student can compose his own poetry. Use the language pattern in the poem to prepare a modified cloze passage of the poem (a cloze passage is one in which some of the words in a phrase or sentence have been blanked out; children fill in the missing words using the meaning or context of the sentence):

Who has seen the wind?

I have, said _____

_____

_____

Discuss how the student might rephrase the poem and generate a list of possible rhyming words to use. When the child has finished the poem, have him read it to you. The poem can be kept in the student's tutoring folder.

Choral Reading

CHORAL READING IS the oral reading of poetry or other texts that makes use of contrasts, sound effects, noises, asides, and movement. Tutors can use choral reading techniques with their students to increase their enjoyment as they learn. In the March 1992 article "Using Choral Reading to Promote Language Learning for ESL Students," Joyce K. McCauley and Daniel S. McCauley suggest ways to help second-language students and other at-risk readers gain understanding and fluency during unison-reading experiences. Because choral reading involves repeated readings, it increases reading rate and decreases the number of mistakes students make when reading out loud. Using the procedures outlined, choral reading can be not only a fun experience, but also one that improves diction, increases vocabulary, and decreases mistakes.

Strategies

Selecting and Preparing Poems

Use poems that are short, simple, and entertaining. Look for poems that rhyme and have rhythm. Choose poems in which action or lines can be inserted to help clarify vocabulary:

> Jack fell down and broke his crown.
> Ouch! (Hold your head.)

Good sources for poems are books by Jack Prelutsky, Karla Kuskin, and Shel Silverstein.

Procedures for Choral Reading

1. Give a quick, engaging introduction of the poem, having the child discuss the main ideas.

2. Read the poem aloud using expression, sound effects, and movement.

3. Give the child a copy of the poem.

4. Read the poem again, letting the child follow along. If needed, point to the words as you read them.

5. Read the poem with the child several times. After several readings, encourage the student to add movements and sound effects of his own.

Figuring Out Words

Using Sound Awareness
from "Phonemic Awareness Helps Beginning Readers Break the Code" by Priscilla L. Griffith and Mary W. Olson

Phonics Instruction
from "Saying the P Word: Nine Guidelines for Exemplary Phonics Instruction" by Steven A. Stahl

Improving Reading Through Meaningful Writing
from "Interactive Writing in a Primary Classroom" by Kathryn Button, Margaret J. Johnson, and Paige Furgerson

Helping Children Recognize Words Using Specific Reading Strategies
from "Moving Learners Toward Independence: The Power of Scaffolded Instruction" by Penny L. Beed, E. Marie Hawkins, and Cathy M. Roller

Word Detectives
from "Procedures for Word Learning: Making Discoveries About Words" by Irene W. Gaskins, Linnea C. Ehri, Cheryl Cress, Colleen O'Hara, and Katharine Donnelly

Invented Spelling and Decoding
from "Making Words: Enhancing the Invented Spelling-Decoding Connection" by Patricia M. Cunningham and James W. Cunningham

Using Sound Awareness

PHONEMIC AWARENESS IS knowing that words are composed of many spoken sounds. Research has found that children with phonemic awareness ability are likely to learn to read more easily than children without this ability. Phonemic awareness does not involve relating sounds to corresponding letters; it merely enhances the ability to learn letter-sound relations. Phonemic awareness is a precursor to learning sound-symbol relations in phonics instruction. It involves rhyming words, blending together sounds of words, and segmenting the sounds of words. In the March 1992 article "Phonemic Awareness Helps Beginning Readers Break the Code," Priscilla L. Griffith and Mary W. Olson give examples of sound-symbol activities that tutors can use with their students.

Strategies

Rhyming

The best way to help young children develop phonemic awareness is by playing with language sounds in meaningful ways. Books and poems including rhyme are natural resources for developing this skill. Some explicit instruction can be useful as well.

➤ Sing songs and recite jingles and poems that include rhymes. Discuss the rhymes you sang and changed.

➤ Read books that include rhyming language, such as *Green Eggs and Ham* or *The Old Lady Who Swallowed a Fly*. Talk about the rhyming words in the book and make up some more.

➤ Prepare a list of 20 pairs of easy words and choose rhyming words for at least half the pairs (for example, *fat-cat*). Explain to the child that rhymes are words that sound the same, and show with examples that some words rhyme and others do not. Say each pair of words and ask the child if they rhyme.

Hearing Sounds in Words

➤ One fun way to hear sounds in words and segment them is to physically depict them through clapping, stamping, or nodding one's head. Say words with one, two, and three syllables and ask children to clap how many sounds they hear after each word that you say.

➤ Engage children in blending words. Prepare a list of 10 short words with 3 or 4 letters. Divide the words before the vowel (for example, *m-an*). Tell the children you will say the words in a secret language and then they are to guess what the words are. Pronounce the *m* alone and then the *an*. Ask the child if she can figure out what the word is by taking the two sounds you made and putting them together. Do the first few words together and then let the child do the rest alone or with a friend.

Phonics Instruction

PHONICS IS A strategy that involves learning the alphabetic principal of language and knowledge of how letters and sounds relate. In the April 1992 article "Saying the P Word: Nine Guidelines for Exemplary Phonics Instruction," Steven A. Stahl discusses ways to teach children using phonics. When children learn sound-symbol relations it helps them to become more independent readers. Learning to recite the rules of phonics is not very useful for children when trying to figure out words, nor are multiple worksheets that have them circle abstract letters and sounds. Phonics is just one small part of the skills involved in learning to read. It is important to spend some time with it in tutoring, but not most or all of your time.

Strategies

Some ideas for tutors that have been found to be helpful when working with phonics are listed following.

➤ Select books that are easy to read and have a predictable story line. These are especially useful for helping children to recognize words.

➤ Use written whole words to teach phonics, and words that come from books that you are reading so they have some contextual meaning. For example, when reading *Polar Bear, Polar Bear What Do You See?*, show the word *bear* and then

teach the sound of the letter *b*. Point out that *bear* begins with the letter *b* which makes the /b/ sound. By introducing *b* or any other letter, the tutor goes directly to the central concept that a letter in a word represents a specific sound and that words come from books that have stories attached. The tutor also can reverse the exercise by showing the letter *b*, then the word *bear*. After this, the child should practice reading words that have the letter *b*, because children learn to read by reading words in stories or in lists.

➤ Find books that repeat letters such as *Pink Pig's Picnic* or a collection of books that feature a letter, such as *The Pet Show*, *Peter Rabbit*, or *Petunia*. Then focus on learning and reinforcing this new sound.

➤ Teach onsets, more commonly called initial consonants or the first letter in a word, and then attach it to a rime, more commonly called a word family. Familiar endings of words are also helpful in teaching relations between letters and sounds. Pieces of words in word families are quite regular in our language. Provide a child with word families for her to create new words by adding a letter at the beginning. Nearly 500 words can be made from the word families shown in Figure 1.

Figure 1

Word Families for Creating New Words

ack	ain	ake	ale	all	ame
an	ank	ap	ash	at	ate
aw	ay	eat	ell	est	ice
ing	ink	ip	ir	ock	oke
ick	ide	ight	ill	in	ine
op	or	ore	uck	ug	ump

Improving Reading Through Meaningful Writing

ONE WAY TO encourage children to read is to have them work with writing they do themselves, often called "experience stories." These activities are especially useful to tutors who may not have access to a wide variety of reading materials. In their March 1996 article "Interactive Writing in a Primary Classroom," Kathryn Button, Margaret J. Johnson, and Paige Furgerson propose a writing strategy for improving literacy. In interactive writing, children write words in a story about their own experience or interests and the tutor scaffolds the children's thinking about letters in the words (see page 56 for more information on scaffolding). An interactive writing lesson, in addition to providing meaningful reading material, provides many opportunities to teach directly about letters and sounds in words.

Strategies

1. The child and the tutor decide on a topic for writing. This is usually tied to a daily activity. It can be an experience, a list of characters from a story, a favorite part of a story, an invitation to parents, or a letter to a friend. Anything that is interesting or meaningful to the child is acceptable.

2. Ask the child how to begin.

3. The student decides on the first word or sentence.

Words

4. Say the word slowly with the student. The student names the sounds she hears.

5. Use the letter names generated by the child to say the first letter of the word. Ask the child to write the letter.

6. Say the word again with the child and discuss the sounds she hears and what letter would be next. Have the student write the next letter or letters.

7. Continue the procedure until the word or sentence is written.

The tutor can use the following prompts to scaffold the child's thinking about words.

- How many words are there in our sentence?
- Where do we begin writing?
- After writing one word, what do we have to remember to do? Why?
- Say the word slowly. What sounds do you hear?
- Can you write the letter that stands for that sound?
- Can you find the letter on our alphabet chart that we need to write?
- What comes at the end of a sentence?
- Would that make sense?
- Does that look right?
- Would you point and read what we have written so far?

Helping Children Recognize Words Using Specific Reading Strategies

TUTORS OFTEN DO not know how much time they should spend teaching individual words or what kinds of strategies they can use to correct or cue students as they are reading. In their May 1991 article "Moving Learners Toward Independence: The Power of Scaffolded Instruction," Penny L. Beed, E. Marie Hawkins, and Cathy M. Roller propose a method of word support that focuses on the turn-by-turn interactions between children and their tutors. This type of scaffolding is strategic and focuses on figuring out words in context or from the meaning of the text.

Strategies

The scaffolds included here were designed for the Strategic Word Attack Technique (SWAT). There are five sequential steps to SWAT. Tell you students to

1. Read to the end of the sentence.

2. Reread and look at pictures.

3. Ask yourself, "What word that starts with this letter would make sense in this sentence?"

4. Look at the parts of the word and blend them together.

5. Read on or ask for help.

The cues described in these scaffolding tips are all based on using the SWAT strategy, however, they would also apply to other strategies.

➤ *Provide general cues.* These comments provide the least support and are global in their perspective. They include comments like "Are you stuck on that word? What can you try?"

➤ *Cue specific strategies.* Direct the child to think about a specific strategy by referring to its name. For example, "When something doesn't make sense what do you do? Have you tried rereading and looking at the pictures?"

➤ *Cue specific elements.* Direct the child to think about a specific element of the strategy. For example, ask "Did you reread the sentence to figure out what made sense?" or "Did you think about the parts of the word?"

➤ *Invite student performance.* Identify the elements of the strategy and encourage the student to join in the task. For example, "Remember, yesterday we asked ourselves what would make sense and then looked at the parts of the word." Either you or the child responds by saying "We looked at the parts of the word and then put them together." Then you lead the way by saying "Let's say the parts of the word." The student blends the parts and says, "Yes, that makes sense."

➤ *Model.* Model strategic thinking by identifying and naming the elements of the strategy while completing the task. For example, "Let's see, first I think about what would make sense, then I look at the parts of the word and put them together."

In this process, the tutor encourages the child to assume most of the responsibility for figuring out the word. By asking "What are you going to do?" or "What would make sense?" the tutor helps the child to use the SWAT strategy on her own. But if the student pauses and cannot figure out a word, the tutor switches to cueing or modeling.

Word Detectives

IN MANY CLASSROOMS, teachers use lists of key words that all students need to know to read successfully. Tutors can take advantage of the lists to help their students become better readers. Talking to your student's teacher and obtaining a list of key words will provide tutors with another tool to use in their sessions. In the December 1996/January 1997 article "Procedures for Word Learning: Making Discoveries About Words," Irene W. Gaskins, Linnea C. Ehri, Cheryl Cress, Colleen O'Hara, and Katharine Donnelly suggest a structured "word detective" program that uses key words. Children are taught a strategic process of using these words to figure out unfamiliar words.

Strategies

1. Discuss the reasons for learning about words with your student. Talk about various strategies for word learning:

- Show the student how she associated the word *cat* with a picture. This is called visual-cue reading.
- Tell your student that we sometimes use some visual cues and some letter-sound cues, for example figuring out *kitten* by the thinking of the sounds of /k/ and /n/ and by associating the word with a picture.
- Tell her that we sometimes use all the letters and sounds to figure out a word, for example using /k/-/a/-/t/ to figure out *cat*.

2. Model how to talk about the letters and sounds and the list of key words you have gotten from your student's teacher. (You can write the list on a large piece of paper to refer to during your tutoring session.)

> (Pointing to a key word) First, we stretch out the word so we can hear all the sounds. As I hear a sound, I hold up a finger. Next, we look at the word and count the letters. Then, we figure out what letters go with what sounds.

3. The child then practices using the self-talk you have modeled using the keywords and the Talk-to-Yourself chart in Figure 2.

You can look for books that contain the key words, including those with rhyming patterns found in the key word list. The child can read these books before or after doing the activity described in

---

Figure 2

Talk-to-Yourself Chart

1. The word is _____.
2. Stretch the word.
    I hear _____ sounds.
3. I see _____ letters because _____.
    (Student reconciles the number of letters he or she sees with the number of sounds he or she hears.)
4. The spelling pattern is _____.
5. This is what I know about the vowel: _____.
6. Another word in the key word list with the same vowel sound is _____.

---

this section. At the end of the session, have the child restate what key words she has learned. You also can extend the lesson by allowing the student to take home the book and the list of key words to work with her parents.

Invented Spelling and Decoding

AS YOUNG CHILDREN read, they develop new ways of figuring out unfamiliar words. They begin to use familiar words and their letter patterns to spell and decode (or read) words. In the October 1992 article "Making Words: Enhancing the Invented Spelling-Decoding Connection," Patricia M. Cunningham and James W. Cunningham present a strategy tutors can use to help beginning readers develop their ability to spell words and apply this knowledge when decoding. In this procedure, children learn to make a six- or seven-letter word from smaller words. This activity is used along with other writing activities to increase students' decoding ability.

Strategies

Planning the Lesson

This lesson will take some planning. You will want to use words your student knows from reading you have done together.

1. Decide on the final word in the lesson—the "long word" you want the student to learn.

Words

2. Make a list of the shorter words that can be made from the letters of the final word. You should try to use words from material the student has read.

3. From all the words listed, pick 12 to 15 words. You will want to include words that can be sorted for the patterns; words of different lengths so that the lesson provides both challenging and easy work; words that can be made with the same letters, for example *barn* and *bran*; a proper name so the student can be reminded to use capital letters; and words with familiar meanings.

4. Write all the words on cards and order them from shortest to longest.

5. Then order the words to emphasize letter patterns.

6. Store the cards in an envelope. Write the list of words in the order you will have the student spell them on the envelope.

Teaching the Lesson

1. Place the larger letter cards in a pocket chart on an easel or along the chalk ledge of a chalkboard.

2. Give a set of letters to the child.

3. Hold up and name the letters on your large letter cards, and have the child hold up her matching small letter cards.

4. Write the number 2 on the board to tell her to take two letters and make the first word. Say the word and then use it in a sentence.

5. Once a child has made the word correctly, have her make the word in the pocket chart using the bigger letters.

6. Continue having the student make words. Be sure to indicate the number of letters needed for each word. Cue the student as to whether she is changing one letter, changing several, or using all the letters to make a word.

7. Before telling her the last word, ask if she has figured out how to make a word with all the letters. Then have her make the last word.

8. Review all the words in the lesson, saying and spelling each word in the lesson order. Point out letter patterns.

9. Use the patterns to spell a few new words.

A Beginning Making Words Lesson

Give the student the vowel letter *i* (make the vowel a different color from the other letters) and the consonant letters *g*, *n*, *p*, *r*, and *s*. Here is a possible set of steps to follow:

1. Take two letters and make *in*.

2. Add a letter to make the three-letter word *pin*.

3. Change just one letter and turn your *pin* into a *pig*.

4. Now change just one letter and your *pig* can become a *rig*. Sometimes we call a big truck a *rig*.

5. Let's make one more three-letter word, *rip*.

6. Now let's make a four-letter word. Add a letter to *rip* and you will have *rips*.

7. Change just one letter and you can change your *rips* to *nips*—sometimes a very young puppy nips at your feet.

8. Now, and this is tricky, do not add any letters and do not take any away. Just change the order of the letters and you can change *nips* to *spin*.

9. There is one more word that you can make with these same four letters. Move your letters one more time and change *spin* to *pins*.

10. Let's make two more four-letter words. Use four letters to make *sing*.

11. Now change just one letter, and change *sing* to *ring*.

12. Now we will make a five-letter word. Add a letter to change *ring* to *rings*.

13. Can you figure out what word we can make with all six letters?

14. Take all six of your letters and make *spring*.

You can then draw your student's attention to the words she made and help her sort for a variety of patterns, such as words that use the same four letters or words that have more than one letter before the vowel.

SECTION V

Supporting Understanding

Introducing a Storybook
from "Introducing a New Storybook to Young Readers"
by Marie M. Clay

Scaffolds for Comprehending
from "Literacy Scaffolds: Strategies for First- and Second-
Language Readers" by Owen F. Boyle and
Suzanne F. Peregoy

Visual Mapping
from "Story Map Instruction: A Road Map for Reading
Comprehension" by Zephaniah T. Davis and
Michael D. McPherson

Prereading Strategies
from "Developing Disadvantaged Children's Background
Knowledge Interactively" by Katherine Maria

Literature Webbing
from "Using a Literature Webbing Strategy Lesson With
Predictable Books" by D. Ray Reutzel and
Parker C. Fawson

Using Students' Experience to Develop Writing Strategies
from "Comprehending and Composing Through Language
Experience" by Mary F. Heller

Introducing a Storybook

LIKE EVERYONE ELSE, children are uncomfortable and sometimes even afraid of things that are new to them. Taking the time to introduce a new book to a child can increase his interest in reading it. In the December 1991 article "Introducing a New Storybook to Young Readers," Marie M. Clay discusses how tutors can develop a context for reading a new story. She believes that giving children a rich introduction instead of simply reading the whole story from start to finish with no time spent discussing the book first is helpful for children who want to read independently. The tutor can anticipate what might be difficult for the child, but at the same time maintain a conversational interchange about the story.

Strategies

When introducing a book, tutors can use a variety of strategies:

➤ Invite the child to respond to the new book by looking at the illustrations and thinking about other similar stories.

➤ Invite the child to share an experience that would be similar to the story.

➤ Sketch the plot up to the climax, leaving the surprise untold in order to create a framework for anticipating what will occur.

➤ Develop understanding around the theme of the book. Explain any concepts or plot twists that might be confusing to the child.

➤ Restate or expand the child's statements in order to maintain the interaction.

➤ Prompt the child using a variety of questions and pauses such as the following:

1. Link information from the pictures to the child's personal knowledge. Use questions such as, "Have you ever done that?"

2. Pause for the child to generate an ending. The pause indicates to the child that he is to finish telling what might happen.

3. Encourage reflection by asking questions such as, "How did you know that?" This encourages children to consider what they are thinking.

➤ Accept partially correct responses. Use what the children say to expand and elaborate the story rather than correcting or rejecting a response. For example say, "I like the way you thought about x, but did you notice...?"

➤ Probe to find out what the child knows. For example ask, "Do you know x?" or "Have you ever seen x?"

➤ Mention new knowledge that may be problematic for the child. Use a particular phrase, explain a particular segment while looking at a picture, or contrast something with a familiar story.

➤ Because you want the child to be active, suggest that the child to link new knowledge with things he already knows. For example, "There is a cat in the picture. Do you or your friends have a cat? Does it look like this cat?"

➤ Model by intentionally saying one particular sentence pattern two or three times to familiarize the child with the language pattern as well as the phrasing and intonation.

Scaffolds for Comprehending

AS DEFINED IN Section II (see page 24), scaffolding is expanding on a child's learning through modeling, questioning, or feedback. Scaffolding is a useful technique for tutors to use because it helps them to enable their students to think on their own both in and out of the tutoring session. In their November 1990 article entitled "Literacy Scaffolds: Strategies For First- and Second-Language Readers," Owen F. Boyle and Suzanne F. Peregoy suggest that comprehension can be enhanced through scaffolds provided by text and by tutors. Examples of scaffolding include beginning a sentence in a familiar book and allowing the child to finish it, or asking the child to write a rhyming book after you have read several such books together.

Strategies

Patterned Reading and Writing

Books that make use of repeated sentence or word patterns are excellent resources for scaffolding. These include repetitive poems or stories such as *Green Eggs and Ham* by Dr. Seuss. When the tutor reads the repeated pattern, the child can easily chime in on the repeated phrases. The repeated phrases make learning to read easier.

After reading the book or poem several times on his own, the child can experiment with writing his own books and poems using sentence patterns. For example, you might encourage your student to write poems using the phrases "I used to be...but now I am..." and "I am the one who..." over and over with different words filled in by the child.

Story Mapping

Many children's stories have a basic structure: one or two major characters, a goal one character wishes to achieve, an obstacle, and a resolution of the conflict between goal and obstacle. A simple story map can help students focus their attention on the parts of a story. You can use the story map in Figure 3 to encourage your student to think in new ways about a story you have read together. The steps for using a story map are as follows:

1. Introduce the story-map frame included in Figure 3.

2. Read a story aloud, for example, *Little Red Riding Hood.*

3. Have the child complete the map using one of the characters. For example, a child who selects the wolf as the character might come up with "The Wolf/wanted to eat Little Red Riding Hood/but the woodcutter killed him/so Little Red lived happily ever after."

Figure 3
A Story-Map Frame

Someone	wants	but	so

4. Have the child share his map with you, summarizing the story orally.

5. The child also can illustrate the map.

Directed Reading Thinking Activity (DRTA)

The DRTA shows children how expert readers question themselves as they read and predict what will happen next. To use this strategy, begin by discussing a story's topic before you read it. Introduce ideas or vocabulary that may be new and set a purpose for reading. Once you have done this, encourage the child to ask questions about the story, and ask him to predict what will happen or give any information he may know. Accept predictions without judgment. After reading the selection, ask the child to verify predictions.

Visual Mapping

ANOTHER METHOD OF using story mapping is described in the December 1989 article "Story Map Instruction: A Road Map for Reading Comprehension." Authors Zephaniah T. Davis and Michael D. McPherson suggest using mapping strategies to help children organize story content into a coherent whole. They focus on using modifications of a spider-style map rather than the traditional linear form of a map found in Figure 3. The figures in this section illustrate maps that tutors can use to work with their students.

Strategies

Story-Map Construction

1. You should create the story map prior to your lesson with the student. Begin story-map construction by brainstorming a list of possible story elements. This list may include themes, settings, characters, events, actions, consequences, and reactions. The examples included here were created using the story in Figure 4 on page 60.

2. Create a list of main ideas, major events, and principal characters. Arrange the list in some kind of order, for example chronologically. Figure 5 on page 61 contains an organized list.

3. Select the type of story map you will use. Examples and descriptions of the different kinds of maps are provided later in this section, but Figure 6 on page 63 contains the basic format.

4. Place the main idea in the predominant bubble on map. For example, in Figure 6, the main idea "Mike Muddle middle Muddle" is in the center and all other information about the story flows out from this idea.

5. Place second-level information, such as settings or main characters on the ties projecting from the main idea. This information is not as important as the main idea, but is still critical to the story. For example, in Figure 6, chronology is the secondary information.

6. Place third-level information in a clockwise sequence around the second-level information. Third-level information is the details about the story. In Figure 6, this includes the secondary characters.

Figure 4

Summary of "The Middle Muddle"

At lunch Mike Muddle began making tracks in the potatoes with his fork. "Mike!" said Mrs. Muddle. "You're too old to play with your food."

Mike's older brother, Steve, pushed back his chair. "I have to get packed for our campout."

Mike asked, "Can I go with Steve?"

"No," his mother sighed. "You're too young to go camping."

Now it was Mike's turn to sigh. Everybody considered him either too small or too big to do what he wanted.

That afternoon, Mike decided to weed the tomato patch. Down at the end of the street, three men were digging a hole. "I can weed a tomato patch any day," Mike thought as he walked to the corner. "But it isn't every day that I can watch men digging a hole right in the middle of the street."

"Hello there, young fellow," said a red-haired workman.

Mike smiled. "Say, does that kitten belong to one of you?" he asked.

"Where? I don't see any…" The workman looked around just in time to see the tip of a tail disappear into a narrow pipe.

"We've got to get that cat out," shouted one of the workmen.

"The water's going to be turned on in less than two minutes."

Mike could hear the kitten's frightened meowing. "We can't let the kitten drown!" he cried out in alarm. "We have to get it out!"

A workman lay flat on the ground and put his hand into the pipe. "I can't reach the kitten," sighed the man. "My arm's too big."

"Let the boy try," shouted someone in the group which had gathered to watch. "His arm's thin so it won't scrape the sides of the pipe."

Mike put his arm into the pipe. Suddenly he felt soft fur touch his fingertips. Carefully he pulled the kitten toward him. A loud cheer came from the group.

Then Mike thought of something. If he had been little, he would have been taking a nap. If he had been old, he would have been camping.

"Know what?" he whispered to the kitten. "It's a good thing I'm the middle Muddle."

Figure 5

List of Attributes Brainstormed for "The Middle Muddle"

Main idea
> Sometimes it is difficult being the middle child in a family, or being at an in-between age or size. However, we are all important regardless of birth order, age, or size; there are advantages and disadvantages to each circumstance.

Characters
> Mike Muddle
> Mike's mother
> Susie, Mike's younger sister
> Steve, Mike's older brother
> Workmen
> Kitten
> Bystanders

Settings
> Kitchen/dining area in Muddle home
> Garden in Muddle yard
> Construction site on Muddle street

Events (actions, reactions, consequences)
> Mike is told that he is too old to play with his food like his sister, Susie.
> Mike is told that he is too young to go camping like his older brother, Steve.
> Steve goes camping.
> Susie takes a nap.
> Mike weeds tomatoes.
> Workmen work on water mains.
> Mike watches workmen.
> Workmen tease Mike about his name.
> Kitten enters water pipe.
> Workmen cannot remove kitten.
> Mike removes kitten.
> Bystanders and workmen cheer for Mike.

Story-Map Instruction

Students need to be taught how to use story maps. The map should be introduced with questions:

- What do you think the story is about?
- Who do you think is the first character in the story? Why?
- Who is the most important character?
- What do you know about the story?

You also can ask questions about setting, events, or actions.

After you have discussed the story map with your student, tell the student to read the story to see how accurate his guesses are. Tell him to change the guesses where it is appropriate. The reading can be done orally or silently. Make sure you guide the student to look at the story map occasionally as he reads to check predictions and summarize.

Various types of story maps that can be used for different purposes are presented in the discussion that follows.

➤ *Inferential story map.* These maps are used to help children recognize text information and then use that information to infer unstated ideas. Students read to verify, modify, or elaborate inferences and supply the missing information. For example, in Figure 7 on page 64, students need to combine explicit information such as, "too old for baby activities" with what they know about this type of information to infer how Mike feels about it. To use an inferential map, have the child think about what he knows and his personal feelings or interpretations of the textual information to infer the missing information.

Figure 6

Literal Story Map for "The Middle Muddle"

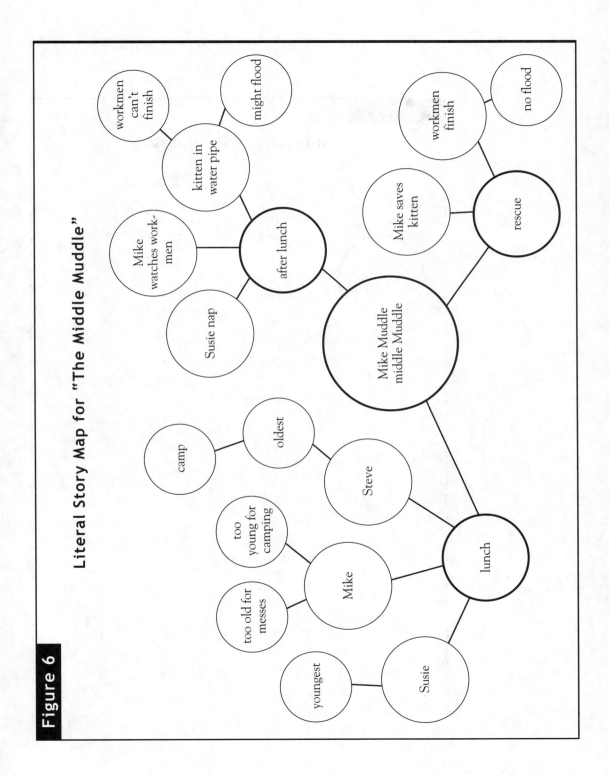

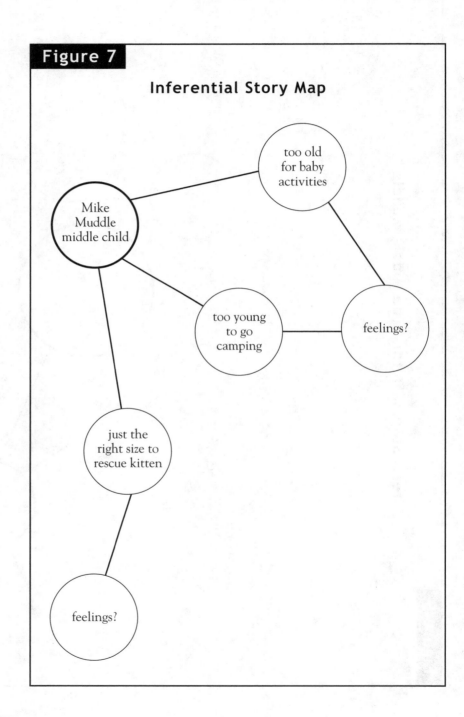

Figure 7

Inferential Story Map

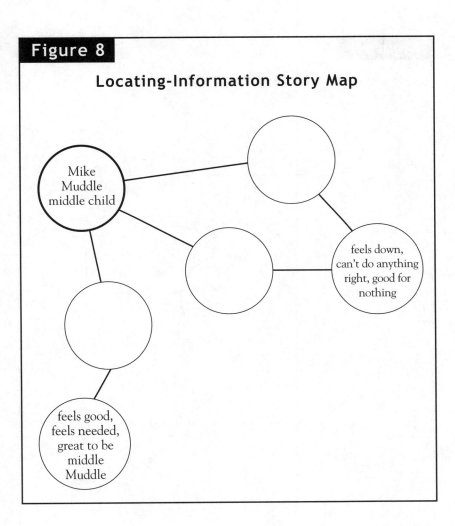

Figure 8

Locating-Information Story Map

Mike
Muddle
middle child

feels down,
can't do anything
right, good for
nothing

feels good,
feels needed,
great to be
middle
Muddle

▶ *Locating-information story map*. This type of map asks students to do the opposite of an inferential story map. The student leaves out the information and includes the inference, as in Figure 8. Have your student find information to support the inference.

▶ *Cause-effect story map*. This type of map asks students to link story events into a cause-and-effect chain. Place

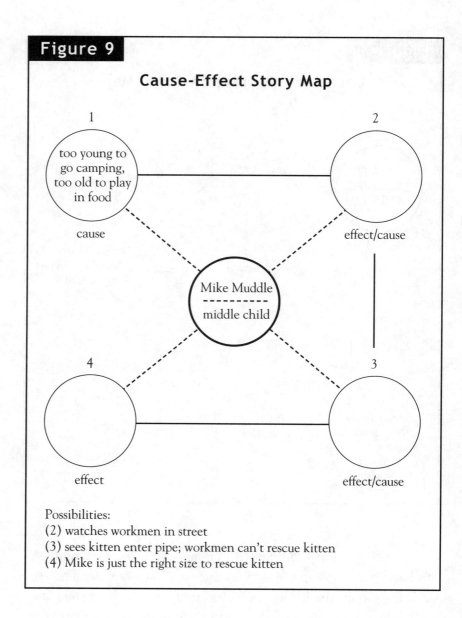

Figure 9

Cause-Effect Story Map

1

too young to
go camping,
too old to play
in food

cause

2

effect/cause

Mike Muddle
- - - - - - - - - -
middle child

4

effect

3

effect/cause

Possibilities:
(2) watches workmen in street
(3) sees kitten enter pipe; workmen can't rescue kitten
(4) Mike is just the right size to rescue kitten

the initial causal event from the story in the first bubble, as in Figure 9. As the child reads or after he or she reads, ask the student to place cause-effect events in the bubbles until reaching the final effect of the initial causal event.

Prereading Strategies

BACKGROUND KNOWLEDGE IS the information about a topic that a reader brings to a text that helps him understand and appreciate it. When developing background knowledge before reading a story, tutors need to focus on the central theme to enhance story understanding. In the January 1989 article "Developing Disadvantaged Children's Background Knowledge Interactively," Katherine Maria reminds tutors to focus on a main theme that might be unfamiliar to the children with whom they are working.

Strategies

Guidelines for Choosing Prereading Strategies

1. Do not always use the same prereading strategies. Try to vary the strategies you use to suit the story, the child's mood, and the tone of the session. Two suggested strategies that work with a variety of texts follow:

- *Semantic mapping* in which the main theme is placed in the center of a circle and the child brainstorms what he knows or predicts about the story as the tutor writes these ideas on lines extending out from the circle; and

- *Experience-Text-Relationship (ETR)* in which interactive tutor-student discussion relates the child's experience to the text's ideas. For example, when reading a story such as *The Three Little Pigs* have your student talk about different kinds of houses and how stable they are. Afterward, talk about the relation among type of house, stability, and planning ahead.

2. Consider the nature of the text and its ideas. Think about the content and style of the book. Is it complicated? Is there a great deal of information that will be new to the child? These factors should affect your choices, which could include the strategies that follow:

- For informational material, K-W-L is most appropriate. This is a strategy in which the child charts what he already *knows*, *wants* to know, and has *learned* in columns on a sheet of paper.
- For stories, use the story-map format (see pages 57 to 66) to introduce the story parts before reading a narrative text.

3. Consider the child's background knowledge. What aspects of the text will be most familiar? Use the following strategies to incorporate background knowledge into prereading:

- Find an anchor point in what the child already knows that can be used to generate ideas related to the main theme of the text.
- Converse about the topic allowing children to make their own connections about the main theme using their background knowledge. Ask questions such as "Have you ever experienced this?"

Literature Webbing

LITERATURE WEBBING IS a visual representation of stories to provide a scaffold for understanding literature. In their December 1989 article "Using a Literature Webbing Strategy Lesson With Predictable Books," D. Ray Reutzel and Parker C. Fawson describe the procedures used in a first-grade classroom. Using the Literature Webbing Strategy Lesson (LWSL) with a predictable book significantly improved young readers' comprehension.

Strategies

Literature webs help children understand that stories have a structure. The steps for creating a web with your student are outlined here. The story used as an example in Figures 10, 11, and 12 on pages 70 to 72 is *How Much Is a Million?* by D.M. Schwartz (1985).

1. Select sections of a predictable book of sufficient length to allow the child to make predictions about the pattern or order of the book.

2. Read these selected sections and show the accompanying pictures to the child in a random order.

3. Place the title of the predictable book in the center of a literature web on a blackboard or piece of paper (see Figure 10 on page 70).

4. The child predicts the order of the book by placing the text excerpts in a clockwise order around the literature web (see Figure 11 on page 71).

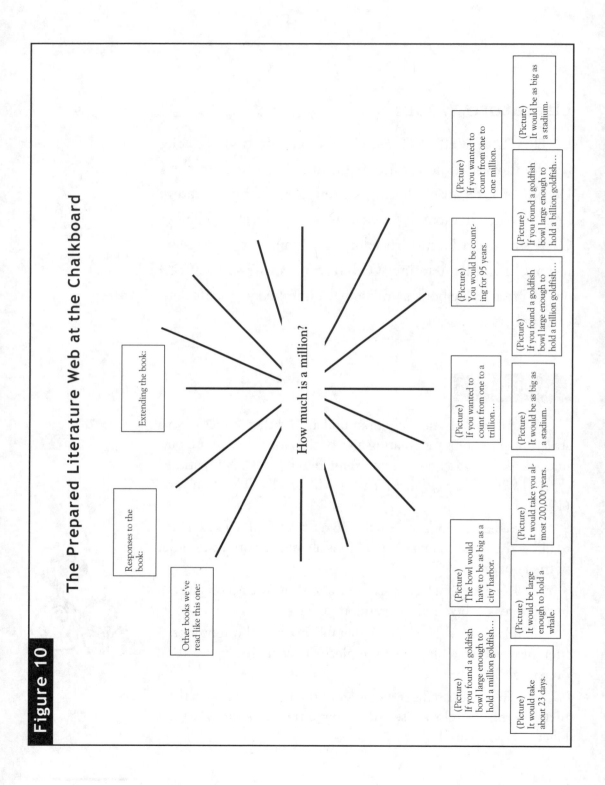

The Prepared Literature Web at the Chalkboard

Figure 10

Responses to the book:

Extending the book:

Other books we've read like this one:

How much is a million?

(Picture)
If you wanted to count from one to one million.

(Picture)
You would be counting for 95 years.

(Picture)
If you wanted to count from one to a trillion...

(Picture)
It would be as big as a stadium.

(Picture)
If you found a goldfish bowl large enough to hold a billion goldfish...

(Picture)
It would be as big as a stadium.

(Picture)
If you found a goldfish bowl large enough to hold a trillion goldfish...

(Picture)
It would take you almost 200,000 years.

(Picture)
The bowl would have to be as big as a city harbor.

(Picture)
If you found a goldfish bowl large enough to hold a million goldfish...

(Picture)
It would be large enough to hold a whale.

(Picture)
It would take about 23 days.

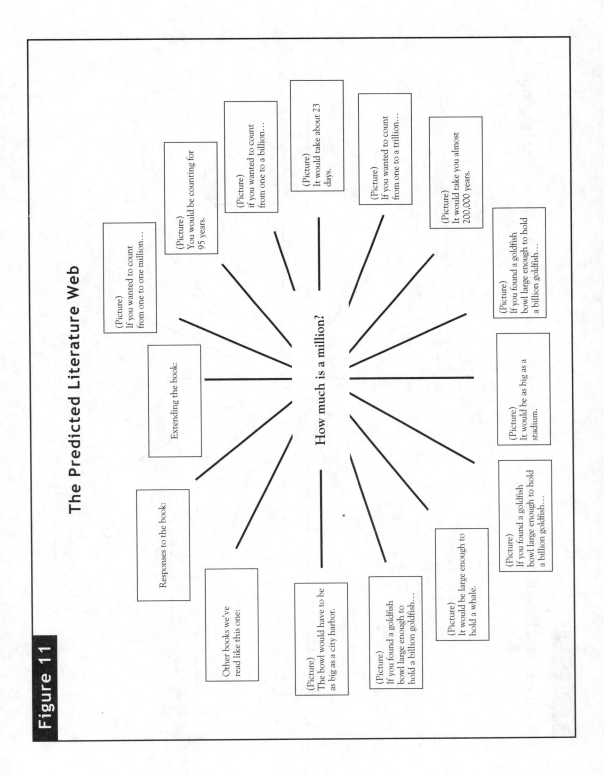

Figure 11

The Predicted Literature Web

How much is a million?

(Picture)
If you wanted to count from one to one million...

(Picture)
You would be counting for 95 years.

(Picture)
if you wanted to count from one to a billion...

(Picture)
It would take about 23 days.

(Picture)
If you wanted to count from one to a trillion...

(Picture)
It would take you almost 200,000 years.

(Picture)
If you found a goldfish bowl large enough to hold a billion goldfish...

(Picture)
It would be as big as a stadium.

(Picture)
If you found a goldfish bowl large enough to hold a billion goldfish...

(Picture)
It would be large enough to hold a whale.

(Picture)
If you found a goldfish bowl large enough to hold a billion goldfish...

(Picture)
The bowl would have to be as big as a city harbor.

Other books we've read like this one:

Responses to the book:

Extending the book:

Figure 12

The Confirmed or Corrected Literature Web With Discussion and Extensions

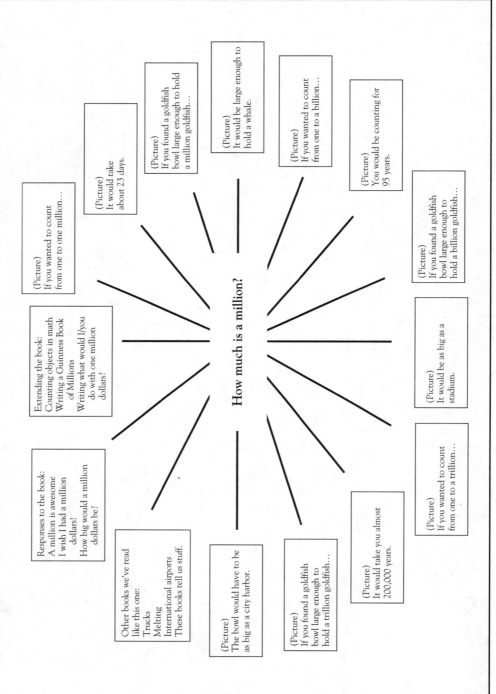

How much is a million?

(Picture)
If you wanted to count from one to one million...

(Picture)
It would take about 23 days.

(Picture)
If you found a goldfish bowl large enough to hold a million goldfish...

(Picture)
It would be large enough to hold a whale.

(Picture)
If you wanted to count from one to a billion...

(Picture)
You would be counting for 95 years.

(Picture)
If you found a goldfish bowl large enough to hold a billion goldfish...

(Picture)
It would be as big as a stadium.

(Picture)
If you wanted to count from one to a trillion...

(Picture)
It would take you almost 200,000 years.

(Picture)
If you found a goldfish bowl large enough to hold a trillion goldfish...

(Picture)
The bowl would have to be as big as a city harbor.

Other books we've read like this one:
Trucks
Melting
International airports
These books tell us stuff.

Responses to the book:
A million is awesome
I wish I had a million dollars!
How big would a million dollars be?

Extending the book:
Counting objects in math
Writing a Guinness Book of Millions
Writing what would I/you do with one million dollars?

5. Read the book with the child chiming in or have the child read silently.

6. The child confirms or corrects his predictions from the reading.

7. The child then responds to three final strands on the literature web: other books like this one, personal response, and extension activities (for example, What else could we do with the information found in this book?) (See Figure 12.)

Literature webs highlight predictable patterns and help children understand the text. After completing the activity together, give the child the option of reading the book on his own, following along as you read it, or writing his own version of the story.

Using Students' Experience to Develop Writing Strategies

OFTEN THE BEST reading material for children is stories about themselves. Language experience techniques help tutors engage students by using the students' stories as reading material. In her November 1988 article "Comprehending and Composing Through Language Experience," Mary F. Heller suggests using language experience along with a story structure framework to help readers develop composing and comprehension. Language experience stories are those dictated by children about experiences they have, stories they know, or stories they create. They are oral language written down.

Prewriting

1. Select a concrete experience that has been decided by the child. Make sure the experience is relevant and important to the student to enhance his interest.

2. Decide on the purpose for writing and limit the topic. For example, are you writing to tell a story, to explain something, or to prove a point?

3. Discuss the audience for the writing. For example, are you writing to parents, classmates, fictional audiences, or perhaps government officials?

4. Read a model story that contains a clear purpose and an easily identifiable audience with your student.

5. As you read the story, point to key features that illustrate the development of the language experience.

6. Have children think about the writing and make some notes about what to include.

Writing and Rewriting

1. As the child dictates the story, help him monitor what he is writing, checking to see if key story elements are included.

2. Talk to your student about what is needed to make the story understandable to the reader.

3. As the story is dictated, it is read, reread, and rewritten. The active nature of composing is emphasized.

Editing

When the story is reread in its draft form, double-check grammar, spelling, and punctuation with the student.

Follow-Up Reading and Writing Activities

After the story is completed, the final story becomes a basis for a reading lesson. Because the child can anticipate the language and language structure, he will read the story more fluently than a book that is less familiar. The student can use the language experience to model his writing a story using the same structure.

Frameworks for Tutoring Young Children to Read

A Tutoring Approach for Children With Reading Problems
from "A Literacy Lesson Framework for Children With Reading Problems" by Susan Tancock

One-on-One Tutoring for First Graders
from "Reading Recovery: Learning How To Make a Difference" by Gay Su Pinnell, Mary D. Fried, and Rose Mary Estice

Teaching Students With Special Needs
from "Classroom Teachers Prevent Reading Failure Among Low-Achieving First-Grade Students" by Barbara M. Taylor, Ruth A. Short, Barbara J. Frye, and Brenda A. Shearer

A Program for Volunteer Tutors
from "A Community Volunteer Tutorial That Works" by Marcia Invernizzi, Connie Juel, and Catherine A. Rosemary

A Tutoring Approach for Children With Reading Problems

TUTORS BRING THEIR unique beliefs and approaches to the tutoring session. However, it also can be helpful to look at the beliefs of those in the literacy field who work with at-risk children. In her October 1994 article "A Literacy Lesson Framework for Children With Reading Problems," Susan Tancock describes her tutoring approach that is based on the belief that all children can learn to read and write when they are asked to use their strengths. This is best accomplished through authentic reading in children's trade books where the tutor relates all activities to a theme. The author provides some specific suggestions to illustrate this approach.

Strategies

Included in the lesson framework are the following suggestions:

➤ *Familiar reading.* Have the student select several familiar books and read aloud to you. Remind the student to read so that the story sounds interesting.

➤ *Guided reading.* This strategy encourages the student to read independently with your help.

1. Select a book that includes familiar topics and that the child will be able to read.

2. Before reading the story, discuss key concepts needed to understand the story.

3. As the student reads orally, prompt her to use several cues (for example, the picture, the overall meaning of the story, or the initial letter of a word) to figure out unfamiliar words.

4. Stop periodically to ask, "What do you think will happen next? Why do you think that?"

5. After the student finishes reading the story, help her to retell or write the story.

➤ *Writing*. Shared writing is a strategy in which the emergent writer generates a message with your support.

1. The child says the words slowly, listening to the sounds, and then writes the sounds.

2. If the child needs help, write a word that rhymes and has the same letters as the target word, then show the child how to use known words to figure out an unknown word when writing.

3. Following the writing, copy the sentence onto a strip of paper, and cut the sentence between each word.

➤ *Word sorting*. Keeping collections of familiar words to sort into categories is a very helpful strategy with students who need to build the number of words they recognize on sight. Collect words during the various activities and place them on cards. Sort the words according to common characteristics. For example, sort words with common spelling patterns, common meanings, or words that belong to the same category, such as food.

➤ *Book sharing*. Read a quality trade book aloud to the child. Focus on relaxing and enjoying the story, letting the child's imagination unfold.

One-on-One Tutoring for First Graders

MANY PROGRAMS EXIST to help at-risk readers. These programs use a variety of different approaches to tutoring. One such program, Reading Recovery, began in New Zealand under the direction of Marie Clay. This intensive first-grade, one-to-one tutoring program includes instructional material such as predictable books that fit the student's instructional level. In their award-winning January 1990 article "Reading Recovery: Learning How To Make a Difference," Gay Su Pinnell, Mary D. Fried, and Rose Mary Estice explain the procedures of Reading Recovery.

Strategies

The format for Reading Recovery is based on several premises:

- All children can become good readers.
- Initial reading instruction must include enormous amounts of reading and writing.
- Teaching builds on each child's strengths, not deficits.
- Instruction must focus on strategies of reading or the "how to" of the reading process.

The lesson format is laid out as follows:

➤ *Reading familiar stories.* Each day the child begins by rereading books that have previously been part of a lesson. This provides an opportunity for the child to engage in fluent reading.

➤ *Taking a running record.* Observe the child as she reads the book that was introduced the previous day. Record miscues and make sure the book fits the student.

➤ *Working with letters.* If a child is just beginning to learn about letters, work briefly each day with plastic letters and a magnetic board. The child begins by spelling her own name and proceeds to spell other familiar words.

➤ *Writing a message or story.* Every day the child composes a brief message of one or two sentences in a special book. The child writes the message on the bottom of the page. The top of the page is called the practice page. The child writes known words and then attempts unfamiliar words with your help. Ask the child to say the sounds slowly and predict what letter might be in the word. Write the word together on the practice page using boxes divided for letter sounds. After the message is written, write it on a sentence strip and cut apart the words. The child should reassemble the sentence and read it as a whole.

➤ *Reading a new book.* Every session introduce the child to a new book by looking at the pictures a page at a time while retelling the story. The child becomes familiar with the plot, important ideas, and some of the language, creating an expectation of the story content and words. The child then reads the book on her own. Provide prompts when necessary.

Teaching Students With Special Needs

ANOTHER SUCCESSFUL INTERVENTION program is called Early Intervention in Reading. In their April 1992 article "Classroom Teachers Prevent Reading Failure Among Low-Achieving First-Grade Students," Barbara M. Taylor, Ruth A. Short, Barbara J. Frye, and Brenda A. Shearer discuss how they worked with first-grade teachers to create this program that targeted the five lowest achieving students in each class and worked with them as a group for 15 to 20 minutes each day. Tutors can use some of these approaches with individual students

Strategies

1. On the first day, read a picture book to your student demonstrating fluent and expressive reading.

2. That same day, read a 40–50 word summary of the book.

3. As you read the story aloud, stop at four or five words and model how to segment them into their sounds and how to blend together the sounds.

4. The child should write five words from the story as you model saying the sounds slowly. The child writes the sounds in a series of boxes duplicated on a sheet of paper, placing one sound in each box.

5. The next time you meet, have the child read the story summary from a chart you have created. The chart should contain an abbreviated version of the story using large print. Try to

include words that are familiar to your student. Provide prompts when necessary.

6. The child will then write a sentence about the story. Guide the writing by hinting at the sounds of words that are unfamiliar.

7. Finally, the child should reread the story summary with you. Encourage the child to use her new strategies to figure out unfamiliar words. After reading the targeted summary, she rereads other familiar books.

8. After the child is comfortable reading the summary, she can take a copy home to read to her parents.

A Program for Volunteer Tutors

A PARTNERSHIP BETWEEN a school system, a university, and the community can be formed to help at-risk children improve their reading and skills. In their December 1996/ January 1997 article "A Community Volunteer Tutorial That Works," Marcia Invernizzi, Connie Juel, and Catherine A. Rosemary explain that the partnership maintains the community's involvement in education for all children by training volunteers from the community and the university.

Strategies

Inherent in the program is a key triad of the child, the volunteer tutor, and the reading coordinator. The reading coordinator works with 15 volunteers at a time, helping each tutor gear word study and new books to a child's level of reading development.

The lesson format is as follows:

Rereading Familiar Books

1. Every tutorial begins with the rereading of three or four familiar books.

2. This session ends with an independent reading of the new book from the previous session.

Word Study

1. The reading coordinator prepares word or picture cards that will enhance the child's understanding about how sounds in words work.

2. With the tutor's help the children initially sort the picture cards by beginning sounds.

3. As these sounds are learned, the tutor introduces more complex word features such as consonant blends and short vowels.

4. Words are put on cards that are used during the tutoring session.

Writing

1. Children are encouraged to compose sentences based on their familiar text. For example, *In a dark, dark room* might become *In a dark, dark house*.

2. As the children write, the tutor helps the child by elongating the sounds in the words so that children can match the letters to the sounds they hear.

3. The tutor helps the child with unfamiliar letter-sounds.

Reading a New Book

1. At each session, the tutor and the child preview a new book and talk about the content. The tutor points out pictures that will correspond to the words on the page.

2. After the preview, the child is encouraged to read the book on her own. If the child hesitates, the tutor supports the child with choral reading.

3. The second reading is done independently and the tutor and child discuss the book again.

Conclusion

BOTH VOLUNTEER TUTORS and teachers play critical roles in helping all students become fluent readers during the early grades. Volunteer tutors need to support the work of trained teachers to help reinforce what has been learned as well as practice what has been taught. Tutors are not the teachers for the children; they add additional support. Tutors are important for the relationships they build with students who have had difficulties both in and out of the classroom. The tutor also can help build a child's self-esteem. Building a warm feeling of trust and making the child feel successful when progress is made are two of the most important things a tutor can do with the child he or she tutors.

Teachers need to discuss with tutors information about the children they tutor. Tutors need to have some knowledge of problems with which a child might need help. Teachers can offer suggestions for working with the child being tutored and provide appropriate materials.

Tutors need to be trained with a series of sessions that talk about the six parts of the tutoring session outlined in *The Reading Team: A Handbook for Volunteer Tutors K–3*.

Tutors need lots of strategies for reading with children, working with words, comprehension, writing, and reading for pleasure. Ongoing training and supervision is a key to a successful program. After they have begun tutoring, tutors can be introduced to even more strategies, such as those offered in this book.

Teachers and trainers of tutors can use this book as a way to help tutors adapt instructional procedures to the particular needs of children with whom they work. Because teachers understand these needs, they are in a position to recommend specific strategies that will increase the learning of specific children. Therefore, it is our hope that teachers and tutor supervisors use this book as they work collaboratively with volunteer tutors to identify the most effective instructional procedures for each child.

Selecting and adapting the articles from *The Reading Teacher* has been a fascinating and worthwhile experience. Although this book includes many instructional procedures that teachers and tutors can use, you also will find more innovative activities within the pages of *The Reading Teacher*. In addition to this and the first publication for the Reading Team, *The Reading Team: A Handbook for Volunteer Tutors K–3*, the International Reading Association has many other publications that can help expand your repertoire of teaching techniques.

Besides techniques, teaching and tutoring require lots of quality, easy-to-read books. Be sure to use the school library, the public library, and other community resources to amass an abundance of books for children to read. One excellent resource is the parents of the children in the school. You could set up a lending library to use in the program by asking parents to donate books and time.

We do believe that trained volunteer tutors can make a difference in helping all students become fluent readers by the end of third grade. We hope this book will add to the training and education of volunteer tutors and teachers who work with children who are struggling to learn to read. Finally, as a tutor, we hope you experience the wonderful feeling of teaching a young child to read. As teachers of young children know, this is a remarkable and rewarding experience.

The Reading Teacher Article Reference List

Barrentine, S.J. (1996). Engaging with reading through interactive read-alouds. *The Reading Teacher, 50,* 36–43.

Beed, P.L., Hawkins, E.M., & Roller, C.M. (1991). Moving learners toward independence: The power of scaffolded instruction. *The Reading Teacher, 44,* 648–655.

Boyle, O.F., & Peregoy, S.F. (1990). Literacy scaffolds: Strategies for first- and second-language readers. *The Reading Teacher, 44,* 194–200.

Button, K., Johnson, M.J., & Furgerson, P. (1996). Interactive writing in a primary classroom. *The Reading Teacher, 49,* 446–454.

Cairney, T., & Langbien, S. (1989). Building communities of readers and writers. *The Reading Teacher, 42,* 560–567.

Clay, M.M. (1991). Introducing a new storybook to young readers. *The Reading Teacher, 45,* 264–273.

Cunningham, P.M., & Cunningham, J.W. (1992). Making words: Enhancing the invented spelling-decoding connection. *The Reading Teacher, 46,* 106–113.

Davis, Z.T., & McPherson, M.D. (1989). Story map instruction: A road map for reading comprehension. *The Reading Teacher, 43,* 232–240.

Dowhower, S.L. (1989). Repeated reading: Research into practice. *The Reading Teacher, 42,* 502–507.

Fielding, L., & Roller, C.M. (1992). Making difficult books accessible and easy books acceptable. *The Reading Teacher, 45,* 678–685.

Gambrell, L.B. (1996). Creating classroom cultures that foster reading motivation. *The Reading Teacher, 50,* 14–23.

Gaskins, I.W., Ehri, L.C., Cress, C., O'Hara, C., & Donnelly, K. (1996–1997). Procedures for word learning: Making discoveries about words. *The Reading Teacher, 50,* 312–327.

Griffith, P.L., & Olson, M.W. (1992). Phonemic awareness helps beginning readers break the code. *The Reading Teacher, 45,* 516–523.

Heller, M.F. (1988). Comprehending and composing through language experience. *The Reading Teacher, 42,* 130–135.

Hough, R.A., Nurss, J.R., & Enright, D.S. (1986). Story reading with limited English speaking children in the regular classroom. *The Reading Teacher, 39,* 510–514.

Invernizzi, M., Juel, C., & Rosemary, C.A. (1996–1997). A community volunteer tutorial that works. *The Reading Teacher, 50,* 304–311.

Klesius, J.P., & Griffith, P.L. (1996). Interactive storybook reading for at-risk learners. *The Reading Teacher, 49,* 552–560.

Maria, K. (1989). Developing disadvantaged children's background knowledge interactively. *The Reading Teacher, 42,* 296–300.

McCauley, J.K., & McCauley, D.S. (1992). Using choral reading to promote language learning for ESL students. *The Reading Teacher, 45,* 526–533.

Oldfather, P. (1993). What students say about motivating experiences in a whole language classroom. *The Reading Teacher, 46,* 672–681.

Pinnell, G.S., Fried, M.D., & Estice, R.M., (1990). Reading Recovery: Learning how to make a difference. *The Reading Teacher, 43,* 282–295.

Rasinski, T.V. (1989). Fluency for everyone: Incorporating fluency instruction in the classroom. *The Reading Teacher, 42,* 690–693.

Reutzel, D.R., & Fawson, P.C. (1989). Using a literature webbing strategy lesson with predictable books. *The Reading Teacher, 43,* 208–215.

Stahl, S.A. (1992). Saying the p word: Nine guidelines for exemplary phonics instruction. *The Reading Teacher, 45,* 618–625.

Strickland, D.S., & Morrow, L.M. (1989). Interactive experiences with storybook reading. *The Reading Teacher, 42,* 322–323.

Strickland, D.S., & Morrow, L.M. (1990). Sharing big books. *The Reading Teacher, 43,* 342–343.

Tancock, S. (1994). A literacy lesson framework for children with reading problems. *The Reading Teacher, 48,* 130–140.

Taylor, B.M., Short, R.A., Frye, B.J., & Shearer, B.A. (1992). Classroom teachers prevent reading failure among low-achieving first-grade students. *The Reading Teacher, 45,* 592–597.

Topping K. (1989). Peer tutoring and paired reading: Combining two powerful techniques. *The Reading Teacher, 42,* 488–494.

Turner, J., & Paris, S.G. (1995). How literacy tasks influence children's motivation for literacy. *The Reading Teacher, 49,* 662–673.

Wicklund, L.K. (1989). Shared poetry: A whole language experience adapted for remedial readers. *The Reading Teacher, 42,* 478–481.